SUMMARY

OF

THE OBESITY CODE

Unlocking the Secrets of Weight Loss

by Jason Fung

A FastReads Book Summary with
Key Takeaways & Analysis

TABLE OF CONTENTS

EXECUTIVE SUMMARY...2
INTRODUCTION..3
PART 1: THE EPIDEMIC..4

HOW OBESITY BECAME AN EPIDEMIC
INHERITING OBESITY

PART 2: THE CALORIE DECEPTION...6

THE CALORIE-REDUCTION ERROR
THE EXERCISE MYTH
THE OVERFEEDING PARADOX

PART 3: A NEW MODEL OF OBESITY..9

A NEW HOPE
INSULIN
CORTISOL
THE ATKINS ONSLAUGHT
INSULIN RESISTANCE: THE MAJOR PLAYER

PART 4: THE SOCIAL PHENOMENON OF OBESITY 14

BIG FOOD, MORE FOOD AND THE NEW SCIENCE OF DIABESITY
POVERTY AND OBESITY
CHILDHOOD OBESITY

PART 5: WHAT'S WRONG WITH OUR DIET? 18

THE DEADLY EFFECTS OF FRUCTOSE
THE DIET SODA DELUSION
CARBOHYDRATES AND PROTECTIVE FIBER
PROTEIN
FAT PHOBIA

PART 6: THE SOLUTION 23

WHAT TO EAT
WHEN TO EAT

EXECUTIVE SUMMARY

In *The Obesity* Code, Dr. Fung debunks old myths we have always believed about weight loss. He argues that obesity is nothing more than a hormonal disorder that can be conquered when we eat in a way that balances the hormones. In a nutshell, Dr. Fung asserts that obesity isn't about exercise or calories or fat grams, but instead, it's only about the hormones.

Insulin – the most discussed hormone in this book – is responsible for regulating our metabolism. In simple terms, when the levels of insulin become too high for prolonged periods of time, people develop an insulin resistance that inevitably makes them fat. Even if you aren't interested in weight loss or type 2 diabetes, this book offers multiple strategies that help the readers understand where they're going wrong with their diet.

INTRODUCTION

For years, you've believed that low-calorie or low-fat diets will magically make you lose weight. In fact, it's widely accepted that if you eat less and exercise more, you're more likely to become slim. But, what if all that's wrong? What if weight loss has nothing to do with calories or fat grams but is only about insulin?

In this book, Dr. Fung relies on his research to argue against the same old myths that have plagued us forever. There is a lot of confusion about weight loss and type 2 diabetes, but instead of addressing the cause, we only think about treating the symptoms. We've all had those days when nothing seems to work even after exercising for countless hours. Many people hope for the best after subscribing to the myth of crash diets, but do they even work? Dieting and exercising seem useless for most of us, yet we see people lose weight effortlessly. So, how does it happen? Well, the answer lies in our hormones.

Additionally, even if you lose weight after dieting, you're not alone when you gain all that weight back when you quit dieting. When weight loss seems like an insurmountable obstacle, many people stop trying. However, this book shows how intermittent fasting can not only help you get back in shape, but your energy and concentration levels will also be better than ever.

Key Takeaways

• Weight loss isn't about low-calorie and low-fat diets, but it's about the insulin levels present in your body.

• Crash diets will make you gain weight after you quit dieting, but intermittent fasting is long lasting, and you'll finally be able to lose all those pounds for good.

PART 1: THE EPIDEMIC

HOW OBESITY BECAME AN EPIDEMIC

With so many myths surrounding us about obesity, it can sometimes get extremely confusing. In fact, many doctors who warn us about the perils of obesity are also overweight. They conclude that it's possible to lose weight by eating less and exercising more, but it simply doesn't work. So, if a doctor's conventional advice is perhaps wrong, then our total understanding about obesity could be wrong too. To lose weight, we must first understand what causes it, rather than following set routines that rarely work.

When dealing with obesity or any other disease, we focus on the proximate cause instead of finding the ultimate cause. For instance, consuming too many calories is only the proximate cause; however, it's not the ultimate one. When you're overweight, you've probably heard people telling you that you that you're lazy or you don't exercise much. Some people will also blame your personal choices because you apparently haven't taken care of yourself. So, as you can see, we try to treat the proximate cause, and although treating the ultimate cause can offer various benefits, unfortunately, we don't do so.

Key Takeaways

• When the AHA announced that people need to consume high carbohydrates with low-fat content, the obesity rates increased dramatically.

• Instead of relying on Mother Nature, we turned our backs on natural fats and consumed more sugar, which made obesity a widespread epidemic.

INHERITING OBESITY

When you look at some families, it's immediately obvious that obese children usually have obese parents. Modern theories blamed environmental factors for this, but when identical twins are adopted and children were tested separately, it was prominent that the children resembled their biological parents, thereby negating the environmental factor theory. This proved that obesity was largely due to an individual's parentage. In simple terms, it means that you inherit obesity. Experts claim that consuming excessive calories can make you obese, but why aren't they considering our inherent genetics?

During the 1970s, the thrifty-gene hypothesis became very popular. For the very first time, the genetic basis related to obesity was observed. The hypothesis concluded that food shortages averted obesity; however, many people have prevented obesity even with an abundance of food. Also, experts fail to recognize the crucial difference between being obese and fat. Think of bears, walruses, and whales for example. Bears fatten regularly before they hibernate because their bodies are designed to do so, but we humans don't do that. While obesity is a state where it presents dangerous health consequences, bears, and whales, although fat, don't face any negative issues.

Key Takeaways

• Obesity is genetic, and although environmental and behavioral factors do contribute to it, they aren't the core of the problem.

• Human evolution favored leanness against obesity.

PART 2: THE CALORIE DECEPTION

THE CALORIE-REDUCTION ERROR

Many people assume that obesity is a result of caloric intake. The first assumption is that they compare calories to thermodynamic equations, which state that the energy that comes in must go out in equal proportions. This means that the calories you consume must be burned, and the excess is apparently stored as fat.

There are many such myths, and though these explanations are intuitive and simple, they are equally dangerous since our body isn't isolated. Just like hormones control our thyroid, circulatory, and every other system, body fat is also regulated. Yet we choose to believe that it's unregulated. Additionally, the number of calories that come in and the amount that go out are independent and don't rely on each other.

Another hazardous assumption is that a calorie, no matter what type, is harmful. This is untrue because the calories found in olive oil, for example, are not the same as the calories in sugar. The common misconception is that weight gain seems to be directly proportional to caloric intake, but studies have shown that people have gained weight even after decreasing caloric consumption. In fact, research has now shown that there is no relation between weight and calories!

Key Takeaways

• Reducing caloric consumption will not help you lose weight since obesity is a hormonal disorder.

• Calories found in different types of food are not the same because they affect our body in various ways.

THE EXERCISE MYTH

During the 1950s, there were many concerns regarding heart disease and obesity, so the new norm was that you could reduce obesity by increasing physical activity. At that point, quite a few gymnasiums popped up, and people were convinced that exercise was the new mantra for weight loss. Governments spent billions of dollars to get people up and running, and even as the rates of physical activity increased, it had no effect on obesity rates at all.

Of course, this doesn't mean that exercising is bad for you, but you'd be ignorant if you believe that exercising will help you burn extra pounds since obesity has no relation to physical activity. Just like a lack of physical activity didn't contribute to obesity, a sudden surge of iron-pumping gyms didn't reduce obesity either. Our body spends energy in several ways such as maintaining the liver, kidney, and brain, and exercising is just one of those factors. However, ignoring other factors and focusing only on physical activity as a magical solution to weight loss is nothing but an erroneous assumption.

Key Takeaways

• Our basal metabolic rate is not constant or stable, and this means that if you reduce the number of calories you take in, then the body will also reduce its energy expenditure proportionally.

• Exercising is certainly important to lead a healthy lifestyle, but it's not the only solution to weight loss.

THE OVERFEEDING PARADOX

Sam Feltham – a personal trainer – experimented on his own body by alternating between a low-carbohydrate and a high-carbohydrate diet that consisted of about 5794 calories per day. He noted that the overfeeding paradox – which stated that calories alone were not responsible for weight gain – completely contradicted the theory of caloric reduction. He gained weight in both the experiments, but the difference was that while the low-carbohydrate diet offered muscle mass, the high-carbohydrate diet was just fat.

During the 1960s, Dr. Ethan Sims performed various experiments related to obesity. He first tried with mice, but later shifted to college students and prisoners. Astonishingly, he found that it was rather difficult to make people obese. Although some gained weight at the beginning of the experiment, they stabilized, and their metabolic rates increased as well. After the tests were stopped, the participants returned to their normal body weight, thereby proving that just like overeating wasn't responsible for permanent weight gain, eating less wouldn't cause weight loss that lasted forever.

Dr. Sims conducted another experiment with two groups of people who were very obese and very lean. The lean people were overfed, and they gained weight while the very obese people reduced their food intake. After a while, both the groups had the same body weight, but remarkably, the originally lean people displayed an increased metabolism whereas the originally very obese people had a reduction in their metabolic rates. In other words, if you eat more calories, your body will also burn more calories resulting in more energy, and an increased metabolism will also shed fat sooner.

Key Takeaways

• Overeating does make you gain weight initially, but your body will stabilize quickly and return to normal once you stop.

• Weight loss depends more on metabolism rather than calories.

PART 3: A NEW MODEL OF OBESITY

A NEW HOPE

When the theory of calorie reduction didn't work, doctors reprimanded and blamed their patients that they weren't following the rules. Increased food consumption didn't lead to obesity, but experts still claimed that a reduction would wipe out obesity. They ignored the hormones completely, but science shows that our body performs just like a thermostat.

Compare the human body with a thermostat trying to regulate the temperature. Imagine that the AC and the heater are both working and are battling it out against themselves. This puts the thermostat under tremendous pressure, and it finally breaks down. Similarly, we fight against our own body to reduce weight, but since our body already has a set body weight like the thermostat with a set temperature, the weight gained or lost will return to normal pretty quickly. Therefore, you tend to gain all the weight you lost even if you've reduced your food consumption, and the opposite is true too. So, how do we find our set body weight? And, most importantly, why is our body weight set to such high levels? Again, the answer lies in the hormones.

Unlike the theory of calorie reduction, the hormonal theory doesn't make false assumptions. Apart from explaining that the amount of calories coming in and going out are not dependent on each other, it also answers how our hormones are responsible for regulating body weight.

Key Takeaways

• When the protein leptin was discovered, scientists believed that they had finally arrived at all the answers related to weight loss, but after it had failed several tests, they realized that it didn't make people obese.

• Obese people are not leptin-deficient; however, they do display leptin resistance.

INSULIN

Coming back to the previous example of comparing the human body with a thermostat, it becomes clear that we need to reduce the set body weight so that the body doesn't fight back to reduce or gain weight. So, how do we reduce the set weight? The answer lies in understanding the most important hormone – insulin.

Various studies have shown that participants gained massive weight whenever they were injected with high doses of insulin. On the other hand, people have also lost weight when the levels of insulin decrease in their body. It's found that obese people have at least 20 percent more insulin when compared to their lean counterparts. Even drugs with more insulin contribute towards obesity and tests revealed that the calories consumed had nothing to do with weight gain. In fact, people became obese even after reducing calories!

It's unknown as to how insulin can cause weight gain, but it's important to understand that it plays a key role in regulating the body weight. As science has already proven that the calories consumed have little to no effects, it's time to understand insulin and treat obesity, which is nothing but a hormonal problem.

Key Takeaways

• People suffering from type 1 diabetes have extremely low levels of insulin, and that's exactly why there's a rapid weight loss.

• Studies have shown that low levels of insulin not only make the applicant lose weight, but it's far more long lasting than dieting and exercising.

CORTISOL

It's already established that insulin increases weight, but one can't ignore the effects of cortisol – the stress hormone – in our body. Cortisol plays a key role in prodding our bodies into action, which means that it increases glucose availability that in turn produces energy to move or run. When you face danger, cortisol ensures that all the energy is used to fight or run, and this short-term increase in cortisol doesn't matter a great deal; however, the problem begins when stress is prolonged for longer periods.

Whether it's related to our professional or personal lives, there's no shortage of stress nowadays. We mostly struggle with emotional problems, and since they don't need any physical activity, the glucose isn't used as energy. This allows the glucose levels to remain high for a long time, which in turn releases more insulin. Obviously, since cortisol increases insulin that leads to weight gain, a reduction would certainly make people lose weight, and studies have proven that participants lost weight as soon as their cortisol levels dropped. In fact, people suffering from Addison's disease have low levels of cortisol, and as expected, they lose weight dramatically.

Key Takeaways

• Sleep deprivation releases more cortisol, and even if you eat less, you're more likely to gain weight if you don't sleep for at least 7-8 hours.

• Sleep deprivation makes you gain weight, but it's not the only factor since it's a combination of various factors including stress that ultimately makes you obese.

THE ATKINS ONSLAUGHT

Now that it's established that insulin causes obesity, it makes sense to understand as to what foods increase the levels of insulin. The culprits are none other than refined carbohydrates, but it also depends on how they are refined. In 1963, Dr. Robert Atkins followed a low-carbohydrate diet to shed weight, and the results were incredible. He even shared his diet plans with his patients, and since they observed rapid weight loss in the initial stages, the Atkins diet became an instant hit.

The AHA, however, stood by its low-fat diet and attacked the credibility of the Atkins diet. Physicians who didn't want to go against the norm argued that the Atkins diet could contribute to risks of heart failure, but the new diet revolution didn't fade because the AHA failed to provide scientific evidence to back their claims. Almost everyone took up the Atkins diet, and although many people lost weight, most people abandoned it within just a year. What was going on?

The Atkins diet encouraged high-fat, low-carbohydrate foods, but it severely restricted foods such as white bread, pasta, chocolate, etc. Most people followed the diet as much as they could, but they gained weight as usual since they couldn't stick to the restrictions anymore. Additionally, a study revealed that people from Asian countries like China and Japan were less prone to obesity although their staple food was rice. When they compared the Asian diet to that of people residing in UK and USA, it was obvious that the Chinese and Japanese consumed less sugar, thereby proving that the key to reducing obesity didn't lie in carbohydrates alone.

Key Takeaways

• The Atkins diet helps reduce weight initially, but after a while, you're likely to gain back all the weight you lost.

• Calories, fats, and carbohydrates don't contribute to obesity, so it's crucial to understand what exactly makes you fat.

INSULIN RESISTANCE: THE MAJOR PLAYER

No matter which diets are prescribed, none of them take time into account even though obesity depends on time. Slowly, we put on at least a kilo each year and then before we know it, we are obese. It's a known fact that higher insulin levels cause weight gain, but we also ignore the importance of insulin resistance.

So, how does one become insulin resistant? The answer is very simple. Just like a cocaine user develops resistance towards the drug after repeated usage, or just like our body resists antibiotics after repeated exposure, we also become insulin resistant when high levels are administered. This also leads to more weight gain. But, high levels can't be blamed alone for resistance. Our body produces hormones in bursts, and the levels drop low again even before we can adjust or develop resistance to it. However, when high levels are combined with a constant stimulus, you can sense trouble on the horizon.

Also, since high insulin levels cause obesity, it becomes even more dangerous when we become resistant to insulin. As the insulin increases, we develop a resistance, and this vicious cycle continues while we're stuck in the middle of it. Obese people with high insulin levels have no choice but to become fatter since they are now resistant to insulin. In other words, this explains homeostasis where the body adjusts itself to react, just like a thermostat.

Key Takeaways

• During the 1960s, people ate white bread and pasta and everything else that increased insulin, but they still didn't become obese since persistently high insulin levels are necessary to become resistant to it.

• Nutritionists now claim that you need to eat at least six meals a day including snacks, but this is theory is not only ridiculous, but it also ruins the balance between an insulin deficient and dominant state.

PART 4: THE SOCIAL PHENOMENON OF OBESITY

BIG FOOD, MORE FOOD AND THE NEW SCIENCE OF DIABESITY

After the AHA had begun accepting money to put its Heart-Check symbol on foods with questionable quality, there was a flood of snack foods on the market. Nobody bothered about the artificial sugars used in these products, and instead of finding a real solution to obesity, they simply blamed calories. Experts also suggested that obese people would lose weight once they consumed more food and this was the biggest myth of all.

Additionally, they also made people believe that a calorie found in any junk food or drink – for instance, a Coke – was equivalent to a calorie found in natural foods like broccoli. Obviously, nobody has grown fat after consuming too many meals of steamed broccoli, but we all know what happens when you drink Coke every day. In fact, most health professionals blatantly promote snack foods even though it's almost impossible to become thin by snacking. Even if you eat fewer calories in your subsequent meal, it's not enough to offset the high number of calories found in the snack itself.

Furthermore, experts recommend that you eat a huge meal for your breakfast every day. They say that if you ignore your breakfast, you're more likely to feel ravenously hungry for the rest of the day. However, this idea is a myth as well. For instance, the French regularly avoid breakfast, and it's no secret that they are usually lean people.

The common myth is that our body needs a boost as soon as we wake up, but this is untrue since our body can take care of itself. It releases hormones that boost our body, and we don't necessarily need to stuff ourselves to gain more energy. Also, don't forget that the term breakfast means that you simply need to break your fast after your body has gone through a period of fasting.

Key Takeaways

• Most people don't feel hungry and tend to skip breakfast; however, thanks to the myths that are advertised on the TV and media, they force themselves to eat in the hopes that they will lose weight.

• You don't have to eat if you aren't hungry just because someone told you to do so.

POVERTY AND OBESITY

Statistics show that obesity has increased considerably in America. What's interesting is that some states, such as Texas, have higher obesity rates when compared to others. Also, Mississippi, known as the poorest state, has the highest obesity. One would think that the rich are more obese since they have access to all kinds of rewarding food, but the fact remains that the poor are more obese than the rich. So, why is this happening?

Since the rich can enjoy any sport they want to, you can assume that they are lean; however, exercising doesn't need a lot of money, and you can gain the same results as a rich man going to the gym by walking every day. So, why exactly are the poor more obese? Think of the food available today. Expensive foods such as steak and cheese are healthy, but since the poor can't afford them, they stick to refined carbohydrates that are not only cheap but are dangerously unhealthy too.

Also, the government recommends a low-fat diet, and even though the poor can include inexpensive foods like legumes and tofu in their diet, they don't do so. Also, one needs to consider the government subsidies for each type of food. Corn – refined into corn syrup and other variants with excess sugar – receives the highest subsidy, and so it wouldn't be wrong to say that the government policy is also a direct cause for obesity.

Key Takeaways

• Sugar was very expensive in the 1920s, and incredibly, the rich were more obese than the poor because they could afford it.

• Many people blame their lifestyle and the advent of cars and computers when they become obese, but the truth is that insulin causes obesity.

CHILDHOOD OBESITY

Obesity not only affected adults, but it didn't spare children either. With type 2 diabetes and obesity rising alarmingly in children, the government spent millions of dollars to manage the situation. Again, people were told to eat as less and exercise more. They even conducted a test where 50 percent of students were obese; however, the results were disappointing, and this strategy seemed useless too.

What is alarming is that childhood obesity continues to adulthood, and although it can be reversed later, the mortality risks can't be ignored. An even more shocking fact is that obesity targets infants too! Since it's a common norm that you must exercise more and eat less, how do we explain the obesity when it comes to infants? The calorie-reduction theories can't answer questions related to this finding since they still believe that depletion in calories will eliminate obesity.

Many hypotheses blame chemicals in the environment, but as obesity is a disorder of the hormones, this theory doesn't even make sense. Again, the answer lies in insulin. Just like high insulin levels affect adults, the same pattern occurs with children. Since the infants inherit this from their mothers, it's easy to understand why infants are sometimes obese.

Key Takeaways

• A mother and infant share the same supply of blood, and thus, the infant inherits high insulin levels from the mother.

• Many studies have confirmed that calories have nothing to do with obesity; however, most of us still believe in myths rather than facing the facts.

PART 5: WHAT'S WRONG WITH OUR DIET?

THE DEADLY EFFECTS OF FRUCTOSE

China had just a mere 1 percent of people with diabetes in the 70s, but now they have shockingly overtaken even America. The Chinese usually consume rice as their staple food, and since it was prevalent even in yesteryears, refined carbohydrates can't take the blame alone. The problem lay in sugar consumption. When companies manufacturing soda couldn't woo the Americans anymore, they shifted their focus to the Asian countries to make up for lost profits, and the results are right in front of our eyes.

Also, the deadly effects of fructose are often ignored. Fructose is found in fruits and is natural, and when we eat fruits, we only gain about 20 grams of fructose per day. However, if you increase fructose levels by consuming concentrated foods such as corn syrup, the problem begins. Companies favored fructose mainly because it was inexpensive compared to sucrose.

Additionally, fructose had several benefits and was the perfect partner for processed foods. It's not only better than glucose since it's sweeter, but it also mixes well in foods, thereby making it the best component in food. Unfortunately, nobody bothered to examine its detrimental effects, and this contributed more to obesity.

Key Takeaways

• Fructose may seem perfect because it's natural and doesn't even raise insulin levels; however, the liver experiences tremendous pressure whenever you consume it.

• High fructose consumption leads to a fatty liver that in turn leads to insulin resistance.

THE DIET SODA DELUSION

With sugar increasing obesity and heart risks, artificial sweeteners made their way into the market. Studies found that Aspartame posed cancer risks in animals, but it was approved despite the warning signs. Later, sucralose replaced Aspartame, and many diet sodas contain this dangerous chemical. People assumed that since diet sodas had no sugar with fewer calories, it was safe for consumption.

After a while, natural sweeteners like Agave nectar and Stevia gained some recognition, but people quickly discarded Agave nectar since it contained at least 80 percent fructose. Experts now recommended that diabetic patients could use artificial sweeteners in their diet since it was a safer alternative to sugar. But, was that true? A lack of evidence didn't evoke many questions either, but the fact remains that diet drinks don't help at all. Even when people drank these so-called safe options, obesity and diabetes continued to rise.

Researchers conducted several tests to see if the artificial sweeteners reduced weight, but not only did it not lessen weight, it actually made people fatter! Further studies were even more alarming since they discovered that these sweeteners also posed risks related to the heart. Sure, these chemicals don't contain sugar or calories, but they increase insulin levels, which in turn increases obesity.

Key Takeaways

• Artificial sweeteners not only elevate weight, but they also increase your cravings.

• No matter what you're led to believe, artificial sweeteners pose several problems that aren't related to obesity alone.

CARBOHYDRATES AND PROTECTIVE FIBER

After the Atkins diet had changed everything about how people perceived food, everybody blamed the carbohydrates. Yes, insulin causes obesity and refined carbohydrates are responsible for spiking insulin levels, but does it mean that all types of carbohydrates including natural, unrefined foods are bad? No, this is just a myth again. Take wheat for example. For years, it has been the staple food of America, but now it's considered as the food responsible for causing celiac disease, thanks to its gluten content.

Also, problems begin when you consume foods in their concentrated form. For instance, if you have five oranges, you're not going to able to eat them all in one go. However, it's pretty easy to drink a glass of juice containing five oranges. Similarly, the problem doesn't lie in wheat, but the way they process it that makes the difference. Over the years, wheat has been refined to such an extent that it's stripped of all its goodness, and the remaining flour is immediately absorbed into our bloodstream. However, studies have repeatedly suggested that wheat protects us from diabetes and obesity, and this is only due to fiber.

Key Takeaways

• Fiber can make our food less palatable, and it's also believed that you can reduce obesity by chewing your food as much as possible.

• Fiber is the best tool to fight obesity since it reduces food intake and keeps the levels of insulin very low.

PROTEIN

When there is an imbalance of macronutrients like carbohydrates, proteins, and fats in our body, our diet is thrown off balance, and we suffer from many issues. Nutrients such as omega 6, omega 3, and amino acids are essential for our body since we cannot synthesize them. However, essential sugars and essential carbohydrates don't exist as we don't need them to survive. Basically, carbohydrates are very nutritious, and low-carbohydrate diets seem unbalanced, but they aren't unhealthy.

The Atkins diet later went through a transformation. It was now a new kind of diet that recommended foods that were high in protein and low in carbohydrates and fat. Egg-white omelets and boneless chicken were now more appealing, but protein shakes and bars replaced them quickly. But, the experts realized later that dietary proteins, just like refined carbohydrates, could raise insulin levels considerably.

Key Takeaways

• An individual's blood sugar is identical whether glucose is administered orally or intravenously; however, the levels of insulin differ greatly. Insulin levels spike up when glucose is consumed orally.

• High-protein foods don't contain as many calories, but they still raise the insulin levels.

FAT PHOBIA

Dr. Ancel Keys observed during World War II that the Americans suffered from high risks of heart disease even when they received better nourishment when compared to people in Europe. He declared that the high levels of blood cholesterol were responsible for these heart problems. However, this myth changed later when people realized that cholesterol wasn't akin to sludge forming in a pipe. In fact, if you stop consuming foods with cholesterol, the liver will simply manufacture more.

In an attempt to classify foods, nutritionists divided them into three categories of macronutrients namely proteins, fats, and carbohydrates. Fats were further divided into saturated, trans and unsaturated fats while the carbohydrates were grouped as complex and simple carbohydrates. This analysis was simplistic and easy to understand, but it didn't quite do justice to our complex system that involves hundreds of phytochemicals and nutrients required to regulate the metabolism.

Key Takeaways

• Avocado was considered a bad food because of its fat content, but it's now regarded as a super food, which makes it obvious that all foods with high-fat content aren't necessarily bad.

• Butter and other animal fats are considered dangerous, but they are certainly safer than deadly foods like margarine.

PART 6: THE SOLUTION

WHAT TO EAT

When you take any conventional diets like the Atkins, Mediterranean or even the low-calorie diet into consideration, it's clear that you can lose weight in any of the diets initially. After a short while, however, most dieters hit a plateau and regain weight again because the body resists weight loss when insulin levels rise. Therefore, it's important to consider both the short and long term aspects of weight loss.

It's also essential to understand that a multitude of factors including calories, carbohydrates, and insulin cause obesity, so you can't focus on just a single factor. Like a cardiovascular disease that is a result of family history, gender, age, smoking and several other problems, obesity also occurs when a combination of several factors are at play.

Key Takeaways

• Instead of focusing only on low carbohydrates, calories or fat in your diet, you can try a combination of them all.

• The key to treat obesity is to understand why you're obese in the first place, which means that if you lack sleep, you have to change your sleep pattern rather than reducing your sugar intake.

WHEN TO EAT

When we try to address obesity, we only focus on half the problem, which is our diet. Sure, it's important to understand what to eat, but what about the meal timing? With high insulin levels, the body fights weight loss, and you're likely to regain all the weight lost even if you continue eating less. Clearly, just dieting isn't enough because your meal timing could be the missing piece in the puzzle.

Some foods can prevent high insulin levels, but they don't lower them. Therefore, the best solution to reduce insulin is to fast – a remedy that has been followed traditionally for centuries. Intermittent fasting can extend from one day to thirty-six hours, and although many physicians are against it, the health benefits can't be ignored.

Key Takeaways

• The best way to reduce insulin levels is to abstain from food and indulge in intermittent fasting for short periods of time.

• Fasting and starvation are different from one another because while starvation is involuntary, fasting is voluntary, planned and controlled.

Made in the USA
San Bernardino, CA
21 January 2018